HAL•LEONARD
INSTRUMENTAL
PLAY-ALONG

AUDIO
ACCESS
INCLUDED

PLAYBACK+
Speed • Pitch • Balance • Loop

ALTO SAX

THE GREATEST SHOWMAN

Audio Arrangements by Peter Deneff

To access audio visit:
www.halleonard.com/mylibrary
Enter Code
4475-9493-7349-1463

ISBN 978-1-5400-2842-6

HAL•LEONARD®
7777 W. BLUEMOUND RD. P.O. BOX 13819 MILWAUKEE, WI 53213

In Australia Contact:
Hal Leonard Australia Pty. Ltd.
4 Lentara Court
Cheltenham, Victoria, 3192 Australia
Email: ausadmin@halleonard.com.au

Visit Hal Leonard Online at
www.halleonard.com

COME ALIVE

ALTO SAX

Words and Music by BENJ PASEK
and JUSTIN PAUL

FROM NOW ON

ALTO SAX

Words and Music by BENJ PASEK
and JUSTIN PAUL

THE GREATEST SHOW

ALTO SAX

Words and Music by BENJ PASEK,
JUSTIN PAUL and RYAN LEWIS

A MILLION DREAMS

ALTO SAX

Words and Music by BENJ PASEK
and JUSTIN PAUL

NEVER ENOUGH

ALTO SAX

Words and Music by BENJ PASEK
and JUSTIN PAUL

THE OTHER SIDE

ALTO SAX

Words and Music by BENJ PASEK
and JUSTIN PAUL

REWRITE THE STARS

ALTO SAX

Words and Music by BENJ PASEK
and JUSTIN PAUL

Moderately fast

THIS IS ME

ALTO SAX

Words and Music by BENJ PASEK
and JUSTIN PAUL

TIGHTROPE

ALTO SAX

Words and Music by BENJ PASEK
and JUSTIN PAUL